GRILLING
COOKBOOK

Publications International, Ltd.

Pictured on the front cover: Backyard Barbecue Burgers
(page 10).

ISBN: 978-1-4508-9340-4

Library of Congress Control Number: 2014950498

Manufactured in China.

8 7 6 5 4 3 2 1

Microwave Cooking: Microwave ovens vary in wattage. Use the
cooking times as guidelines and check for doneness before adding
more time.

Preparation/Cooking Times: Preparation times are based
on the approximate amount of time required to assemble the
recipe before cooking, baking, chilling or serving. These times
include preparation steps such as measuring, chopping and
mixing. The fact that some preparations and cooking can be done
simultaneously is taken into account. Preparation of optional
ingredients and serving suggestions is not included.

TABLE OF
CONTENTS

BACKYARD BEEF

SESAME-GARLIC FLANK STEAK

MAKES 4 SERVINGS

1 beef flank steak (about 1¼ pounds)
2 tablespoons soy sauce
2 tablespoons hoisin sauce
1 tablespoon dark sesame oil
2 cloves garlic, minced

1. Score steak lightly with sharp knife in diamond pattern on both sides; place in large resealable food storage bag. Combine soy sauce, hoisin sauce, sesame oil and garlic in small bowl; pour over steak. Seal bag; turn to coat. Marinate in refrigerator at least 2 hours or up to 24 hours, turning once.

2. Prepare grill for direct cooking. Remove steak from marinade; reserve marinade.

3. Grill steak, covered, over medium heat 13 to 18 minutes until medium-rare (145°F) to medium (160°F) or to desired doneness, turning and brushing with marinade halfway through cooking time. Discard remaining marinade.

4. Remove steak to cutting board; let stand 5 minutes. Carve across the grain into thin slices.

BEEF SPIEDINI WITH ORZO

MAKES 4 SERVINGS

- 1½ pounds beef top sirloin steak, cut into 1×1¼-inch pieces
- ¼ cup olive oil
- ¼ cup dry red wine
- 2 cloves garlic, minced
- 1 teaspoon dried rosemary
- 1 teaspoon salt, divided
- ½ teaspoon dried thyme
- ½ teaspoon coarsely ground black pepper
- 6 cups water
- 1 cup uncooked orzo
- 1 tablespoon butter
- 1 tablespoon chopped fresh parsley
- Fresh rosemary sprigs (optional)

1. Place steak in large resealable food storage bag. Combine oil, wine, garlic, dried rosemary, ½ teaspoon salt, thyme and pepper in small bowl; pour over steak. Seal bag; turn to coat. Marinate in refrigerator 15 to 30 minutes.

2. Prepare grill for direct cooking. Soak 8 (6- to 8-inch) wooden skewers in water 30 minutes.

3. Bring 6 cups water and remaining ½ teaspoon salt to a boil in small saucepan over high heat. Add orzo; reduce heat and simmer 15 minutes or until tender. Drain orzo; stir in butter and parsley. Keep warm.

4. Remove steak from marinade; discard marinade. Thread steak onto skewers.

5. Grill skewers over medium-high heat 8 to 10 minutes, turning occasionally. Serve with orzo; garnish with fresh rosemary.

CARNE ASADA

MAKES 8 SERVINGS

- ½ cup tequila
- ¼ cup lime juice
- ¼ cup lemon juice
- ¼ cup orange juice
- 1 medium onion, chopped
- ½ teaspoon garlic powder
- 2 teaspoons ORTEGA® Taco Sauce, Hot
- 1 teaspoon black pepper
- 2 pounds skirt steak
- 12 (8-inch) ORTEGA® Flour Soft Tortillas
- 1 cup ORTEGA® Salsa, any variety
- 1 cup ORTEGA® Guacamole Style Dip

MIX tequila, juices, onion, garlic powder, taco sauce and pepper in large bowl. Add steak and turn to coat both sides. Cover and refrigerate 6 to 8 hours, turning steak over occasionally to marinate evenly.

PREHEAT grill. Sprinkle a few drops of water on each tortilla, stack and wrap in aluminum foil. Place on grill to warm.

REMOVE meat from marinade, reserving marinade. Place on grill. Brush steak with marinade. Cook 12 to 15 minutes for medium-rare (or cook until desired doneness); turn steak and tortillas once during cooking. Remove tortillas from grill. Discard remaining marinade.

TRANSFER steak to cutting board. Cut into thin slices. Serve with tortillas, salsa and guacamole.

TIP: For additional smoky flavor, try grilling the tortillas before serving them with carne asada.

BACKYARD BARBECUE BURGERS

MAKES 6 SERVINGS

1½ pounds ground beef

⅓ cup barbecue sauce, divided

1 onion, cut into thick slices

1 tomato, sliced

2 tablespoons olive oil

6 Kaiser rolls, split

6 leaves green or red leaf lettuce

1. Prepare grill for direct cooking.

2. Combine beef and 2 tablespoons barbecue sauce in large bowl. Shape into six 1-inch-thick patties.

3. Grill patties, covered, over medium heat 8 to 10 minutes (or uncovered 13 to 15 minutes) until medium (160°F) or to desired doneness, turning occasionally. Brush both sides with remaining barbecue sauce during last 5 minutes of cooking.

4. Meanwhile, brush onion and tomato slices with oil. Grill onion slices about 10 minutes and tomato slices 2 to 3 minutes.

5. Just before serving, place rolls, cut side down, on grid; grill until lightly toasted. Serve burgers on rolls with tomato, onion and lettuce.

STRIP STEAKS WITH CHIMICHURRI

MAKES 4 SERVINGS

Chimichurri (recipe follows)

- 4 bone-in strip steaks, 1 inch thick (8 ounces each)
- ¾ teaspoon salt
- ¾ teaspoon ground cumin
- ¼ teaspoon black pepper

1. Prepare grill for direct cooking. Oil grid. Prepare Chimichurri. Sprinkle both sides of steaks with salt, cumin and pepper.

2. Grill steaks, covered, over medium-high heat 8 to 10 minutes until medium-rare or to desired doneness, turning once. Remove to cutting board; let stand 5 minutes before slicing. Serve with Chimichurri.

CHIMICHURRI

MAKES ABOUT 1 CUP

- ½ cup packed fresh basil leaves
- ⅓ cup extra virgin olive oil
- ¼ cup packed fresh parsley
- 2 tablespoons packed fresh cilantro
- 2 tablespoons lemon juice
- 1 clove garlic
- ½ teaspoon salt
- ½ teaspoon grated orange peel
- ¼ teaspoon ground coriander
- ⅛ teaspoon black pepper

Combine all ingredients in food processor or blender; process until smooth.

CHIPOTLE-RUBBED FLANK STEAK

MAKES 4 TO 6 SERVINGS

- 1 packet (1.25 ounces) ORTEGA® Chipotle Taco Seasoning Mix, divided
- ½ cup water
- ¼ cup REGINA® Red Wine Vinegar
- 1½ to 2 pounds flank steak
- 1 tablespoon olive oil
- 1 small onion, diced
- 1 tablespoon ORTEGA® Fire-Roasted Diced Green Chiles
- 1 cup ORTEGA® Garden Salsa

Juice from ½ lime

COMBINE half of seasoning mix, water and vinegar in shallow dish. Add steak and turn to coat well. Marinate 15 minutes in refrigerator. Turn over and marinate 15 minutes longer.

HEAT oil in small saucepan over medium heat. Add onion; cook and stir 5 minutes or until translucent. Stir in chiles and salsa; cook and stir over low heat 5 minutes.

SPRINKLE remaining seasoning mix over both sides of steak. Grill or broil steak over high heat 5 minutes on each side, or to desired doneness. Let stand 5 minutes before slicing against grain. To serve, drizzle on sauce and lime juice.

TIP: For a less formal meal, create flavorful tacos instead. Simply serve the steak and sauce in soft tortillas, and garnish with shredded lettuce, diced tomatoes and shredded cheese, if desired.

CLASSIC CALIFORNIA BURGERS

MAKES 4 SERVINGS

2 tablespoons FRENCH'S® Honey Dijon Mustard

2 tablespoons mayonnaise

2 tablespoons sour cream

1 pound ground beef

2 tablespoons FRENCH'S® Worcestershire Sauce

1⅓ cups FRENCH'S® Cheddar or Original French Fried Onions, divided

½ teaspoon garlic salt

¼ teaspoon ground black pepper

4 hamburger rolls, split and toasted

½ small avocado, sliced

½ cup sprouts

1. Combine mustard, mayonnaise and sour cream; set aside.

2. Combine beef, Worcestershire, ⅔ *cup* French Fried Onions and seasonings. Form into 4 patties. Grill over high heat until juices run clear (160°F internal temperature).

3. Place burgers on rolls. Top each with mustard sauce, avocado slices, sprouts and remaining ⅔ *cup* onions, dividing evenly. Cover with top halves of rolls.

BBQ CHEESE BURGERS: Top each burger with 1 slice American cheese, 1 tablespoon barbecue sauce and 2 tablespoons French Fried Onions.

PEPPERCORN STEAKS

MAKES 4 SERVINGS

- 2   tablespoons olive oil
- 1   to 2 teaspoons cracked pink or black peppercorns or ground black pepper
- 1   teaspoon dried herbs, such as rosemary or parsley
- 1   teaspoon minced garlic
- 4   boneless beef top loin (strip) or rib-eye steaks (6 ounces each)
- ¼   teaspoon salt

1. Combine oil, peppercorns, herbs and garlic in small bowl. Rub mixture on both sides of steaks. Place on plate; cover and refrigerate 30 to 60 minutes.

2. Prepare grill for direct cooking.

3. Grill steaks over medium heat 10 to 12 minutes until medium-rare (145°F) to medium (160°F) or to desired doneness, turning once. Season with salt.

GRILLED SKIRT STEAK FAJITAS

MAKES 4 SERVINGS

1½ pounds skirt steak

½ cup pale ale

3 tablespoons lime juice

1 teaspoon ground cumin

2 tablespoons olive oil

1 cup thinly sliced red onion

1 cup thinly sliced red and green bell peppers

2 cloves garlic, minced

3 plum tomatoes, each cut into 4 wedges

1 tablespoon reduced-sodium soy sauce

¾ teaspoon salt

¼ teaspoon black pepper

8 (7-inch) flour tortillas

Avocado slices and salsa (optional)

1. Place steak in large resealable food storage bag. Combine ale, lime juice and cumin in small bowl; pour over steak. Seal bag; turn to coat. Marinate in refrigerator 2 hours, turning occasionally.

2. Heat oil in large nonstick skillet over medium-high heat. Add onion; cook and stir 2 to 3 minutes or until beginning to soften. Add bell peppers; cook and stir 7 to 8 minutes or until softened. Add garlic; cook and stir 1 minute. Add tomatoes; cook 2 minutes or just until beginning to soften. Add soy sauce; cook 1 minute. Keep warm.

3. Prepare grill for direct cooking. Oil grid. Remove steak from marinade; discard marinade. Sprinkle with salt and black pepper. Grill steak over medium-high heat 4 to 6 minutes per side until 145°F or to desired doneness. Remove to cutting board; let stand 5 minutes. Cut across the grain into ¼-inch slices.

4. Warm tortillas and fill with steak and vegetable mixture. Top with avocado and salsa, if desired.

PATIO PORK & LAMB

THAI-STYLE PORK CHOPS WITH CUCUMBER SAUCE

MAKES 4 SERVINGS

3 tablespoons Thai peanut sauce, divided

¼ teaspoon red pepper flakes

4 bone-in pork chops (5 ounces each)

1 container (6 ounces) plain yogurt

¼ cup diced unpeeled cucumber

2 tablespoons chopped red onion

2 tablespoons finely chopped fresh mint or cilantro

1 teaspoon sugar

1. Combine 2 tablespoons peanut sauce and red pepper flakes in small bowl; brush over both sides of pork chops. Let stand while preparing cucumber sauce, or cover and refrigerate up to 4 hours.

2. Prepare grill for direct cooking.

3. Combine yogurt, cucumber, onion, mint and sugar in medium bowl; mix well.

4. Grill pork, covered, over medium heat 4 minutes; turn and grill 3 minutes or until barely pink in center. Just before removing from heat, brush with remaining 1 tablespoon peanut sauce. Serve with cucumber sauce.

GLAZED HAM AND SWEET POTATO KABOBS

MAKES 4 SERVINGS

- 1 sweet potato (about 12 ounces), peeled
- ¼ cup water
- ¼ cup (½ stick) butter
- ¼ cup packed dark brown sugar
- 2 tablespoons cider vinegar
- 2 tablespoons molasses
- 1 tablespoon yellow mustard
- 1 tablespoon Worcestershire sauce
- ¾ teaspoon ground cinnamon
- ½ teaspoon ground allspice
- ⅛ teaspoon red pepper flakes
- 1 boneless ham slice (about 12 ounces), ¼ inch thick, cut into 20 (1-inch) pieces
- 16 fresh pineapple chunks (about 1 inch)
- 1 package (10 ounces) mixed salad greens

1. Soak 4 (12-inch) wooden skewers in water 20 minutes.

2. Meanwhile, cut sweet potato into 16 pieces; place in shallow microwavable dish with water. Cover and microwave on HIGH 4 minutes or until fork-tender; drain. Spread potatoes in single layer; cool 5 minutes.

3. Combine butter, brown sugar, vinegar, molasses, mustard, Worcestershire sauce, cinnamon, allspice and red pepper flakes in medium saucepan; bring to a boil over medium-high heat. Cook 2 minutes or until reduced to ½ cup. Remove from heat; cool slightly.

4. Prepare grill for direct cooking. Oil grid. Alternately thread ham, sweet potato and pineapple onto

skewers, beginning and ending with ham.

5. Grill skewers over medium heat 6 to 8 minutes or until sweet potatoes are browned and ham is heated through, turning every 2 minutes and brushing with glaze. Cover and let stand 5 minutes.

6. Remove ham, sweet potato and pineapple from skewers; serve over greens.

GREEK LAMB BURGERS

MAKES 4 SERVINGS

¼ cup pine nuts

1 pound ground lamb

¼ cup finely chopped yellow onion

3 cloves garlic, minced, divided

¾ teaspoon salt

¼ teaspoon black pepper

¼ cup plain yogurt

¼ teaspoon sugar

4 slices red onion (¼ inch thick)

1 tablespoon olive oil

8 slices pumpernickel bread

4 slices tomato

12 slices cucumber

1. Spread pine nuts in small skillet. Cook and stir over medium heat 2 minutes or until lightly browned.

2. Combine lamb, pine nuts, chopped onion, 2 cloves garlic, salt and pepper in large bowl; mix well. Shape into 4 patties about ½ inch thick and 4 inches in diameter.

3. Prepare grill for direct cooking. Combine yogurt, sugar and remaining 1 clove garlic in small bowl; mix well.

4. Brush one side of each patty and onion slice with oil; place on grid, oiled sides down. Brush with oil. Grill over medium-high heat, covered, 8 to 10 minutes until medium (160°F) or to desired doneness, turning halfway through grilling. Grill bread 1 to 2 minutes per side during last few minutes of grilling.

5. Serve patties on bread with grilled onion, tomato, cucumber and yogurt mixture.

CUBAN GARLIC LIME PORK CHOPS

MAKES 2 TO 4 SERVINGS

4 boneless pork top loin chops, ¾ inch thick (about 6 ounces each)

2 tablespoons olive oil

2 tablespoons lime juice

2 tablespoons orange juice

2 teaspoons minced garlic

½ teaspoon salt, divided

½ teaspoon red pepper flakes

2 small seedless oranges, peeled and chopped

1 medium cucumber, peeled, seeded and chopped

2 tablespoons chopped onion

2 tablespoons chopped fresh cilantro

1. Place pork in large resealable food storage bag. Combine oil, lime juice, orange juice, garlic, ¼ teaspoon salt and red pepper flakes in small bowl; pour over pork. Seal bag; turn to coat. Marinate in refrigerator up to 24 hours.

2. Combine oranges, cucumber, onion and cilantro in medium bowl; toss gently. Cover and refrigerate 1 hour or overnight. Add remaining ¼ teaspoon salt just before serving.

3. Prepare grill for direct cooking. Remove pork from marinade; discard marinade.

4. Grill pork 6 to 8 minutes per side or until no longer pink in center. Serve with salsa.

HERBED LAMB CHOPS

MAKES 4 TO 6 SERVINGS

8 lamb loin chops, 1 inch thick
   (about 4 ounces each)

⅓ cup vegetable oil

⅓ cup red wine vinegar

2 tablespoons soy sauce

1 tablespoon lemon juice

3 cloves garlic, minced

1 teaspoon salt

1 teaspoon chopped fresh oregano *or*
   ¼ teaspoon dried oregano

1 teaspoon dried rosemary

1 teaspoon ground mustard

½ teaspoon white pepper

1. Place lamb in large resealable food storage bag. Combine oil, vinegar, soy sauce, lemon juice, garlic, salt, oregano, rosemary, mustard and pepper in medium bowl; mix well. Reserve ½ cup marinade in small bowl; pour remaining marinade over lamb. Seal bag; turn to coat. Marinate in refrigerator at least 1 hour.

2. Prepare grill for direct cooking. Remove lamb from marinade; discard marinade.

3. Grill lamb over medium-high heat 4 minutes per side or until desired doneness, basting frequently with reserved ½ cup marinade. Do not baste during last 5 minutes of cooking. Discard any remaining marinade.

STICKY BBQ RIBS

MAKES 4 SERVINGS

- 3 to 3½ pounds pork baby back ribs (2 racks)
- ¾ cup molasses
- ⅓ cup whole grain or spicy brown mustard
- 1½ tablespoons cider vinegar
- ½ tablespoon dry mustard
- ½ teaspoon seasoned salt

1. Prepare grill for direct cooking. Cut each rack of ribs into three pieces.

2. Combine molasses, whole grain mustard, vinegar, dry mustard and seasoned salt in medium bowl; mix well.

3. Grill ribs, meat side up, over medium-high heat about 1 hour and 15 minutes or until tender, turning and brushing frequently with molasses mixture during last 15 minutes of cooking.

BALSAMIC GRILLED PORK CHOPS

MAKES 2 SERVINGS

- 2 boneless pork chops (4 ounces each)
- 2 tablespoons balsamic vinegar
- 2 tablespoons reduced-sodium soy sauce
- 1 teaspoon Dijon mustard
- 2 teaspoons sugar
- ⅛ teaspoon red pepper flakes

1. Place pork in large resealable food storage bag. Combine vinegar, soy sauce, mustard, sugar and red pepper flakes in small bowl; mix well. Reserve 1 tablespoon marinade for serving; pour remaining marinade over pork. Seal bag; turn to coat. Marinate in refrigerator 2 hours or up to 24 hours.

2. Prepare grill for direct cooking. Remove pork from marinade; discard marinade.

3. Grill pork over medium-high heat about 5 minutes per side or until barely pink in center. Drizzle with reserved 1 tablespoon marinade.

MIXED GRILL KABOBS

MAKES 6 TO 8 SERVINGS

- 1 pound boneless beef sirloin, cut into 1-inch cubes
- 2 large red, orange or yellow bell peppers, cut into chunks
- 12 strips bacon, blanched*
- 12 ounces smoked sausage or kielbasa, cut into ½-inch slices
- 1 cup peeled pearl onions or red onion chunks
- 1 pound pork tenderloin, cut lengthwise in half, then into ¼-inch wide long strips
- 1 cup pineapple wedges
- 1½ cups CATTLEMEN'S® Award Winning Classic Barbecue Sauce

To blanch bacon, place bacon strips into boiling water for 1 minute. Drain thoroughly.

1. Arrange beef cubes and 1 bell pepper on metal skewers, weaving bacon strips around all. Place sausage, 1 pepper and onions on separate skewers. Weave strips of pork on additional skewers with pineapple wedges.

2. Baste kabobs with some of the barbecue sauce. Cook on well-greased grill over medium-high direct heat, basting often with remaining barbecue sauce.

3. Serve trio of kabobs with additional sauce.

TIP: To easily cut pork, freeze about 30 minutes until very firm.

NOTE: You may substitute CATTLEMEN'S® Authentic Smoke House or Golden Honey Barbecue Sauce.

MOROCCAN-STYLE LAMB CHOPS

MAKES 4 SERVINGS

- 1 tablespoon olive oil
- 1 teaspoon ground cumin
- 1 teaspoon ground coriander
- ¾ teaspoon salt
- ⅛ teaspoon ground cinnamon
- ⅛ teaspoon ground red pepper
- 4 center-cut lamb loin chops, 1 inch thick (about 4 ounces each)
- 2 cloves garlic, minced

1. Prepare grill for direct cooking.

2. Combine oil, cumin, coriander, salt, cinnamon and red pepper in small bowl; mix well. Brush mixture over both sides of lamb. Sprinkle with garlic.

3. Grill lamb, covered, over medium heat 5 minutes per side until medium or to desired doneness.

PORK TENDERLOIN FAJITAS

MAKES 6 SERVINGS

- 1 pork tenderloin (about 1½ pounds)
- 1 packet (1.25 ounces) ORTEGA® Fajita Seasoning Mix
- ¾ cup water
- 2 tablespoons olive oil
- 1 red bell pepper, cut into thin strips
- 1 green bell pepper, cut into thin strips
- 1 onion, cut into thin strips
- 1 can (4 ounces) ORTEGA® Fire-Roasted Diced Green Chiles

  Juice from ½ lime
- 12 (8-inch) ORTEGA® Flour Soft Tortillas

CUT pork down the middle lengthwise almost completely through, but not severed.

BLEND seasoning mix and water in shallow dish. Add pork and turn to coat. Cover and marinate 30 minutes in refrigerator.

HEAT oil in medium skillet over medium heat until hot. Add bell peppers and onion. Cook and stir 7 minutes or until tender and soft. Stir in chiles.

PREHEAT grill until piping hot, about 15 minutes. Grill pork 4 minutes on each side. Squeeze lime juice over pork and rest 5 minutes; slice pork thinly on the bias.

WRAP tortillas in paper towels and microwave on HIGH (100% power) 1 minute. To assemble fajitas, wrap pork and vegetables in warm tortillas.

NOTE: This pork filling also can be used for tacos or as a topping on crunchy tortilla pizzas.

ITALIAN SAUSAGE AND PEPPERS

MAKES 4 SERVINGS

4   links hot or sweet Italian sausage

1   large onion, cut into rings

1   large bell pepper, cut into quarters

½   cup olive oil

¼   cup red wine vinegar

2   tablespoons chopped fresh parsley

1   tablespoon dried oregano

2   cloves garlic, crushed

1   teaspoon salt

1   teaspoon black pepper

Horseradish-Mustard Spread (recipe follows)

1. Place sausages, onion and bell pepper in large resealable food storage bag. Combine oil, vinegar, parsley, oregano, garlic, salt and black pepper in small bowl; pour over sausage and vegetables. Seal bag; turn to coat. Marinate in refrigerator 1 to 2 hours.

2. Prepare Horseradish-Mustard Spread. Prepare grill for direct cooking. Remove sausage, onion and bell pepper from marinade; reserve marinade.

3. Grill sausage, covered, over medium heat 5 minutes. Turn sausage and place onion and bell pepper on grid; brush with reserved marinade. Discard remaining marinade. Grill, covered, 5 minutes or until sausage is cooked through and vegetables are crisp-tender. Serve with Horseradish-Mustard Spread.

HORSERADISH-MUSTARD SPREAD:
Combine 3 tablespoons mayonnaise, 1 tablespoon chopped fresh parsley, 1 tablespoon prepared horseradish, 1 tablespoon Dijon mustard, 2 teaspoons garlic powder and 1 teaspoon black pepper in small bowl; mix well.

FIRED-UP POULTRY

GRILLED CHICKEN ADOBO

MAKES 6 SERVINGS

½ cup chopped onion

⅓ cup lime juice

6 cloves garlic, coarsely chopped

1 teaspoon ground cumin

1 teaspoon dried oregano

½ teaspoon dried thyme

¼ teaspoon ground red pepper

6 boneless skinless chicken breasts
  (about 4 ounces each)

3 tablespoons chopped fresh cilantro (optional)

1. Combine onion, lime juice and garlic in food processor; process until onion is finely minced. Pour into large resealable food storage bag. Add cumin, oregano, thyme and red pepper; knead bag until blended. Add chicken to bag. Seal bag; turn to coat. Marinate in refrigerator 30 minutes or up to 4 hours, turning occasionally.

2. Prepare grill for direct cooking. Oil grid. Remove chicken from marinade; discard marinade.

3. Grill chicken over medium heat 5 to 7 minutes per side or until no longer pink in center. Sprinkle with cilantro, if desired.

GRILLED CHICKEN TOSTADAS

- 1 pound boneless skinless chicken breasts
- 1 teaspoon ground cumin
- ¼ cup orange juice
- ¼ cup plus 2 tablespoons salsa, divided
- 1 tablespoon plus 2 teaspoons vegetable oil, divided
- 2 cloves garlic, minced
- 8 green onions
- 1 can (16 ounces) refried beans
- 4 (10-inch) *or* 8 (6- to 7-inch) flour tortillas
- 2 cups chopped romaine lettuce
- 1½ cups (6 ounces) shredded Monterey Jack cheese with jalapeño peppers
- 1 ripe medium avocado, diced
- 1 tomato, seeded and diced
  Sour cream (optional)

1. Place chicken in single layer in shallow glass dish; sprinkle with cumin. Combine orange juice, ¼ cup salsa, 1 tablespoon oil and garlic in small bowl; pour over chicken. Cover and marinate in refrigerator at least 2 hours or up to 8 hours, stirring occasionally.

2. Prepare grill for direct cooking. Drain chicken; reserve marinade. Brush green onions with remaining 2 teaspoons oil.

3. Grill chicken and green onions, covered, over medium-high heat 5 minutes. Brush chicken with half of reserved marinade; turn and brush with remaining marinade. Turn green onions; grill, covered, 5 minutes or until chicken is no longer pink in center and green onions are tender.

4. Meanwhile, combine beans and remaining 2 tablespoons salsa in small saucepan; cook over medium heat until hot, stirring occasionally.

5. Place tortillas in single layer on grid. Grill 1 to 2 minutes per side or until golden brown. (If tortillas puff up, pierce with tip of knife.)

6. Remove chicken and green onions to cutting board; let stand 5 minutes. Slice chicken crosswise into ½-inch strips. Cut green onions crosswise into 1-inch pieces. Spread bean mixture over tortillas; top with lettuce, chicken, green onions, cheese, avocado and tomato. Serve with sour cream, if desired.

SMOKED TURKEY BREAST WITH CHIPOTLE RUB

MAKES 8 TO 10 SERVINGS

Mesquite or hickory wood chips

2 tablespoons packed dark brown sugar

2 tablespoons ground cumin

1 tablespoon salt

1 tablespoon garlic powder

1 tablespoon smoked paprika

2 teaspoons ground red pepper

1 teaspoon chili powder

¼ cup (½ stick) butter, softened

1 (5½- to 6-pound) bone-in skin-on turkey breast

1. Prepare grill for indirect cooking. Soak wood chips in water at least 30 minutes.

2. Combine brown sugar, cumin, salt, garlic powder, paprika, red pepper and chili powder in small bowl; mix well. Place 2 tablespoons spice mixture in another small bowl. Add butter; mix well.

3. Gently loosen skin of turkey breast. Spread butter mixture under skin. Rub skin and cavity of turkey with remaining spice mixture.

4. Remove some wood chips from water. Place chips in small aluminum tray. Place tray under grill rack directly on the heat source; allow wood to begin to smolder, about 10 minutes.

5. Grill turkey, covered, over medium-high heat 1 hour. Replenish wood chips after 1 hour. Grill until cooked through (165°F). Remove to cutting board; tent with foil. Let stand 10 minutes before slicing.

MEDITERRANEAN CHICKEN KABOBS

MAKES 8 SERVINGS

- 2 pounds boneless skinless chicken breasts or chicken tenders, cut into 1-inch pieces
- 1 small eggplant, peeled and cut into 1-inch pieces
- 1 medium zucchini, cut into ½-inch slices
- 2 medium onions, each cut into 8 wedges
- 16 medium mushrooms, stemmed
- 16 cherry tomatoes
- 1 cup chicken broth
- ⅔ cup balsamic vinegar
- 3 tablespoons olive oil
- 2 tablespoons dried mint
- 4 teaspoons dried basil
- 1 tablespoon dried oregano

1. Alternately thread chicken, eggplant, zucchini, onions, mushrooms and tomatoes onto 16 metal skewers; place in large shallow dish.

2. Combine broth, vinegar, oil, mint, basil and oregano in small bowl; mix well. Pour mixture over kabobs; cover and marinade in refrigerator 2 hours, turning occasionally.

3. Prepare grill for direct cooking. Remove kabobs from marinade; discard marinade.

4. Grill kabobs over medium-high heat 10 to 15 minutes or until chicken is no longer pink in center, turning halfway through cooking time.

GARLIC & LEMON HERB MARINATED CHICKEN

MAKES 4 SERVINGS

3   to 4 pounds bone-in chicken pieces, skinned if desired

⅓   cup FRENCH'S® Honey Dijon Mustard

⅓   cup lemon juice

⅓   cup olive oil

3   cloves garlic, minced

1   tablespoon grated lemon peel

1   tablespoon minced fresh thyme or rosemary

1   teaspoon coarse salt

½   teaspoon coarse black pepper

1. Place chicken into resealable plastic food storage bag. Combine remaining ingredients. Pour over chicken. Marinate in refrigerator 1 to 3 hours.

2. Remove chicken from marinade. Grill chicken over medium direct heat for 35 to 45 minutes until juices run clear near bone (170°F for breast meat; 180°F for dark meat). Serve with additional mustard on the side.

PREP TIME: 10 minutes
MARINATE TIME: 1 hour
COOK TIME: 45 minutes

TIP: This marinade is also great on whole chicken or pork chops.

BUFFALO CHICKEN DRUMSTICKS

MAKES 4 SERVINGS

- 8 large chicken drumsticks (about 2 pounds)
- 3 tablespoons hot pepper sauce
- 1 tablespoon vegetable oil
- 1 clove garlic, minced
- ¼ cup mayonnaise
- 3 tablespoons sour cream
- 1 tablespoon white wine vinegar
- ¼ teaspoon sugar
- ⅓ cup (about 1½ ounces) crumbled blue cheese
- 2 cups hickory chips
- Celery sticks

1. Place chicken in large resealable food storage bag. Combine hot pepper sauce, oil and garlic in small bowl; pour over chicken. Seal bag; turn to coat. Marinate in refrigerator at least 1 hour or up to 24 hours for spicier flavor, turning occasionally.

2. Combine mayonnaise, sour cream, vinegar and sugar in medium bowl; mix well. Stir in cheese; cover and refrigerate until ready to serve.

3. Soak hickory chips in cold water 20 minutes. Prepare grill for direct cooking. Drain hickory chips; sprinkle over coals. Drain chicken; discard marinade.

4. Grill chicken, covered, over medium-high heat 25 to 30 minutes or until cooked through (165°F), turning occasionally. Serve with blue cheese dressing and celery sticks.

THAI BARBECUED CHICKEN

MAKES 4 SERVINGS

1 cup coarsely chopped fresh cilantro

2 jalapeño peppers,* stemmed and seeded

8 cloves garlic, coarsely chopped

2 tablespoons fish sauce

1 tablespoon packed brown sugar

1 teaspoon curry powder

Grated peel of 1 lemon

3 pounds chicken pieces

*Jalapeño peppers can sting and irritate the skin, so wear rubber gloves when handling peppers and do not touch your eyes.

1. Combine cilantro, jalapeños, garlic, fish sauce, brown sugar, curry powder and lemon peel in food processor or blender; process until coarse paste forms.

2. Work fingers between skin and meat on breast and thigh pieces. Rub about 1 teaspoon seasoning paste under skin on each piece. Rub remaining paste all over chicken pieces. Place chicken in large resealable food storage bag; refrigerate 3 to 4 hours or overnight.

3. Prepare grill for direct cooking.

4. Grill chicken, skin side down, covered, over medium heat about 10 minutes or until well browned. Turn chicken and grill 20 to 30 minutes or until cooked through (165°F). Thighs and legs may require 5 to 10 minutes more cooking time than breasts. (If chicken is browned on both sides but still needs additional cooking, move to edge of grill, away from direct heat, to finish cooking.)

APRICOT COCA-COLA® AND ROSEMARY CHICKEN

MAKES 4 SERVINGS

- 4 boneless skinless chicken breasts
- 2 cloves garlic, minced
- ¼ teaspoon kosher salt
- ¼ teaspoon red pepper flakes
- 4 tablespoons apricot preserves
- ½ cup COCA-COLA®
- ¼ cup low-sodium soy sauce
- 2 tablespoons chopped fresh rosemary, plus additional for garnish

Place chicken in large baking dish. Rub garlic, salt and red pepper flakes over chicken. Spread 1 tablespoon apricot preserves over each chicken breast. Drizzle with *Coca-Cola*® and soy sauce; sprinkle with 2 tablespoons rosemary. Cover and marinate at room temperature at least 30 minutes.

Preheat grill to medium-high heat. Remove chicken from marinade; discard marinade. Grill chicken on lightly greased grill grid coated with nonstick cooking spray 5 minutes on each side or until chicken is cooked through. Serve immediately and garnish with additional rosemary.

CHIPOTLE SPICE-RUBBED BEER CAN CHICKEN

MAKES 4 SERVINGS

2 tablespoons packed brown sugar

2 teaspoons smoked paprika

2 teaspoons ground cumin

1 teaspoon salt

1 teaspoon garlic powder

1 teaspoon chili powder

½ teaspoon ground chipotle pepper

1 whole chicken (3½ to 4 pounds)

1 can (12 ounces) beer

1. Prepare grill for indirect cooking. Oil grid. Pat chicken dry with paper towels.

2. Combine brown sugar, paprika, cumin, salt, garlic powder, chili powder and chipotle pepper in small bowl. Gently loosen skin of chicken over breast, legs and thighs. Rub mixture under and over skin and inside cavity. Discard one fourth of beer. Hold chicken upright with cavity pointing down; set chicken on beer can (so beer can is inside cavity).

3. Place chicken on grid, standing upright on can. Spread legs slightly for support. Grill chicken, covered, over medium heat 1 hour 15 minutes or until cooked through (165°F).

4. Lift chicken off beer can using metal tongs. Remove to cutting board; let stand upright 5 minutes before carving.

SIZZLING SEAFOOD

MUSTARD-GRILLED RED SNAPPER

MAKES 4 SERVINGS

½ cup Dijon mustard

1 tablespoon red wine vinegar

1 teaspoon ground red pepper

4 red snapper fillets (about 6 ounces each)

1. Prepare grill for direct cooking. Oil grid.

2. Combine mustard, vinegar and red pepper in small bowl; mix well. Coat red snapper thoroughly with mustard mixture.

3. Grill fish, covered, over medium-high heat 4 minutes per side or until fish begins to flake when tested with fork.

GRILLED BAJA BURRITOS

MAKES 4 SERVINGS

- 1 pound tilapia fillets
- 6 tablespoons vegetable oil, divided
- 3 tablespoons lime juice, divided
- 2 teaspoons chili powder
- 1½ teaspoons lemon-pepper seasoning
- 3 cups coleslaw mix
- ½ cup chopped fresh cilantro
- ¼ teaspoon salt
- ¼ teaspoon black pepper
  Guacamole and pico de gallo (optional)
- 4 (7-inch) flour tortillas
  Lime wedges (optional)

1. Place tilapia in large resealable food storage bag. Combine 2 tablespoons oil, 1 tablespoon lime juice, chili powder and lemon-pepper seasoning in small bowl; pour over fish. Seal bag; turn to coat. Let stand 10 minutes.

2. Prepare grill for direct cooking. Brush grid with 2 tablespoons oil. Remove fish from marinade; discard marinade.

3. Grill fish over medium-high heat, covered, 3 to 4 minutes per side or until center is opaque.

4. Combine coleslaw mix, remaining 2 tablespoons oil, 2 tablespoons lime juice, cilantro, salt and pepper in medium bowl; mix well.

5. Layer fish, coleslaw mixture, guacamole and pico de gallo, if desired, on tortillas; roll up tightly. Serve with pico de gallo and lime wedges, if desired.

TIP: Any firm white fish, such as snapper or halibut, can be substituted for the tilapia.

BLACKENED CATFISH WITH CREOLE VEGETABLES

MAKES 4 SERVINGS

- ⅔ cup CATTLEMEN'S® Authentic Smoke House Barbecue Sauce or CATTLEMEN'S® Award Winning Classic Barbecue Sauce
- ⅓ cup FRANK'S® REDHOT® Original Cayenne Pepper Sauce
- 2 tablespoons Southwest chile seasoning blend or Cajun seasoning blend
- 1 tablespoon olive oil
- 4 skinless catfish or sea bass fillets (1½ pounds)
  Salt and pepper to taste
  Creole Vegetables (recipe follows)

1. Combine barbecue sauce, FRANK'S RedHot Sauce, seasoning blend and oil. Reserve ½ cup mixture for Creole Vegetables.

2. Season fish with salt and pepper to taste. Baste fish with remaining barbecue mixture.

3. Cook fish on a well-greased grill over medium direct heat 5 minutes per side until fish is opaque in center, turning once. Serve with Creole Vegetables.

CREOLE VEGETABLES

MAKES 4 SERVINGS

- 1 red, green or orange bell pepper, cut into quarters
- 1 large zucchini or summer squash, cut in half crosswise, then lengthwise into thick slices
- 1 large white onion, sliced ½ inch thick
  Vegetable cooking spray

Arrange vegetables on skewers. Coat vegetables with cooking spray. Grill vegetables over medium direct heat until lightly charred and tender, basting often with reserved ½ cup barbecue sauce mixture.

CEDAR PLANK SALMON WITH GRILLED CITRUS MANGO

MAKES 4 SERVINGS

- 4 salmon fillets (6 ounces each), skin intact
- 2 teaspoons sugar, divided
- 1 teaspoon chili powder
- ½ teaspoon black pepper
- ¼ teaspoon salt
- ¼ teaspoon ground allspice
- 2 tablespoons orange juice
- 1 tablespoon lemon juice
- 1 tablespoon lime juice
- 2 teaspoons minced fresh ginger
- ¼ cup chopped fresh mint
- ⅛ teaspoon red pepper flakes
- 2 medium mangos, peeled and cut into 1-inch pieces
- 1 cedar plank (about 15×7 inches, ½ inch thick), soaked*

Soak in water 5 hours or overnight.

1. Rinse salmon; pat dry. Combine 1 teaspoon sugar, chili powder, black pepper, salt and allspice in small bowl. Rub evenly over flesh side of fish.

2. Prepare grill for direct cooking over medium-high heat.

3. Combine remaining 1 teaspoon sugar, orange, lemon and lime juices, ginger, mint and red pepper flakes in medium bowl; mix well.

4. Thread mango pieces onto skewers or spread in grill basket.

5. Turn heat down to medium. Keep clean spray bottle filled with water nearby in case plank begins to burn. If it flares up, spray lightly with water. Oil grid; place soaked plank on top. Cover and heat until plank smokes and crackles. Place fish, skin side down, on plank; arrange mango skewers next to fish.

6. Grill fish and mango, covered, 6 to 8 minutes or until mango is slightly charred, turning frequently. Remove mango from grill. Grill fish 9 to 12 minutes or until fish begins to flake when tested with fork.

7. Remove mango from skewers; add to mint mixture and toss gently to coat. Serve immediately with fish.

TIP: Cedar planks can be purchased at gourmet kitchen stores or hardware stores. Be sure to buy untreated wood at least ½ inch thick. Use each plank for grilling food only once. Used planks may be broken up into wood chips and used to smoke foods.

SURF AND TURF KABOBS

MAKES 4 SERVINGS

1   pound beef tenderloin, cut into 1¼-inch chunks

12 raw jumbo shrimp, peeled and deveined (with tails on)

1   medium onion, cut into 12 wedges

1   red or yellow bell pepper, cut into 1-inch pieces

⅓   cup butter, melted

3   tablespoons lemon juice

3   cloves garlic, minced

2   teaspoons paprika or smoked paprika

½   teaspoon salt

¼   teaspoon black pepper or ground red pepper

Lemon wedges

1. Prepare grill for direct cooking. Oil grid.

2. Alternately thread beef, shrimp, onion and bell pepper onto four 12-inch metal skewers. (Skewer shrimp through ends to form "C" shape for even cooking.)

3. Combine butter, lemon juice, garlic, paprika, salt and black pepper in small bowl; mix well. Brush half of mixture over kabobs.

4. Grill kabobs over medium heat 5 minutes; turn and brush with remaining butter mixture. Grill 5 to 6 minutes or until shrimp are pink and opaque (beef will be medium-rare to medium doneness). Serve with lemon wedges.

TIP: Be sure to purchase jumbo shrimp for this recipe—the shrimp and steak should be approximately the same size so they will cook evenly.

CARIBBEAN GLAZED SWORDFISH WITH GRILLED PINEAPPLE CHUTNEY

MAKES 4 SERVINGS

½ cup FRANK'S® REDHOT® Cayenne Pepper Sauce or FRANK'S® REDHOT® XTRA Hot Cayenne Pepper Sauce

¼ cup packed light brown sugar

1 teaspoon dried thyme leaves

½ teaspoon ground allspice

2 tablespoons olive oil

4 swordfish steaks, 1 inch thick, seasoned with salt and pepper to taste

Grilled Pineapple Chutney (recipe follows)

1. Whisk together FRANK'S Redhot Sauce, sugar, thyme and allspice. Reserve 3 tablespoons mixture for Grilled Pineapple Chutney.

2. Mix oil into remaining spice mixture; thoroughly baste fish.

3. Place fish on well-greased grill. Cook, covered, over medium-high direct heat for 10 to 15 minutes until opaque in center, turning once. Serve with Grilled Pineapple Chutney.

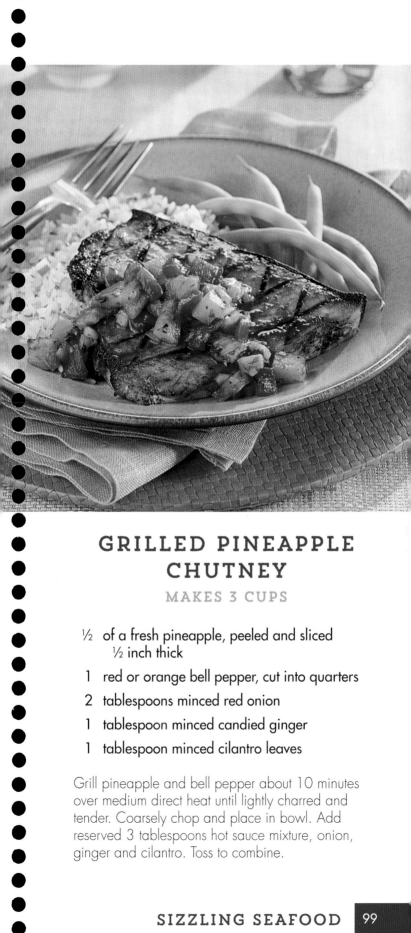

GRILLED PINEAPPLE CHUTNEY

MAKES 3 CUPS

½ of a fresh pineapple, peeled and sliced
½ inch thick

1 red or orange bell pepper, cut into quarters

2 tablespoons minced red onion

1 tablespoon minced candied ginger

1 tablespoon minced cilantro leaves

Grill pineapple and bell pepper about 10 minutes over medium direct heat until lightly charred and tender. Coarsely chop and place in bowl. Add reserved 3 tablespoons hot sauce mixture, onion, ginger and cilantro. Toss to combine.

GRILLED TILAPIA WITH ZESTY MUSTARD SAUCE

MAKES 4 SERVINGS

- 2 tablespoons butter, softened
- 1 teaspoon Dijon mustard
- ½ teaspoon grated lemon peel
- ½ teaspoon Worcestershire sauce
- ½ teaspoon salt, divided
- ¼ teaspoon black pepper
- 4 mild thin fish fillets, such as tilapia (about 4 ounces each)
- 1½ teaspoons paprika
- ½ lemon, cut into wedges
- 2 tablespoons minced fresh parsley

1. Prepare grill for direct cooking. Oil grill basket.

2. Combine butter, mustard, lemon peel, Worcestershire sauce, ¼ teaspoon salt and pepper in small bowl; mix well.

3. Rinse tilapia; pat dry with paper towels. Sprinkle both sides of fish with paprika and remaining ¼ teaspoon salt. Place fish in prepared grill basket.

4. Grill fish, covered, 3 minutes per side or until fish begins to flake when tested with fork. Remove to platter.

5. Squeeze lemon wedges over fish. Spread butter mixture evenly over fish; sprinkle with parsley.

FISH TACOS

MAKES 10 TO 12 TACOS

1   to 1½ pounds firm-fleshed fish fillets, such as red snapper, cut into 4×2-inch strips

2   canned chipotle peppers in adobo sauce, finely chopped

Juice of 2 limes

2   tablespoons chili powder

1   clove garlic, minced

½   teaspoon salt

½   teaspoon black pepper

¼   cup olive oil

½   head red cabbage, shredded

Juice of 1 lemon

½   cup Lime-Cilantro Cream (recipe follows)

8   to 10 flour tortillas

1   cup queso fresco* or feta cheese, crumbled

Queso fresco is a fresh white Mexican cheese available in Latin markets and some large supermarkets.

1. Place fish, skin side down, in large shallow dish. Combine chipotle peppers, lime juice, chili powder, garlic, salt and black pepper in small bowl; whisk in oil. Pour mixture over fish; cover and marinate in refrigerator 1 hour.

2. Meanwhile, combine cabbage and lemon juice in medium bowl; toss to coat. Prepare Lime-Cilantro Cream.

3. Prepare grill for direct cooking. Oil grid.

4. Grill fish, skin side up, 4 to 5 minutes per side or until center is opaque. Remove to plate; let stand 5 minutes. Remove skin from fish; gently break fish into flakes with fork.

5. Place about ¼ cup fish in center of each tortilla. Top with cabbage, cheese and Lime-Cilantro Cream.

LIME-CILANTRO CREAM:

Combine ½ cup fresh cilantro leaves and juice of
2 limes in blender or food processor; blend 1 minute.
Add ¼ cup sour cream; blend until smooth.

SZECHUAN TUNA STEAKS

MAKES 4 SERVINGS

4 tuna steaks, 1 inch thick (6 ounces each)

¼ cup dry sherry or sake

¼ cup soy sauce

1 tablespoon dark sesame oil

1 teaspoon hot chili oil *or* ¼ teaspoon red pepper flakes

1 clove garlic, minced

3 tablespoons chopped fresh cilantro (optional)

1. Place tuna in single layer in large shallow dish. Combine sherry, soy sauce, sesame oil, hot chili oil and garlic in medium bowl; mix well. Reserve ¼ cup soy sauce mixture in small bowl. Pour remaining soy sauce mixture over fish; cover and marinate in refrigerator 40 minutes, turning once.

2. Prepare grill for direct cooking. Oil grid. Drain fish; discard marinade.

3. Grill fish over medium-high heat 3 minutes per side or until seared but still soft in center.* Remove to cutting board; let stand 5 minutes.

4. Cut fish into thin slices. Drizzle with reserved soy sauce mixture; sprinkle with cilantro, if desired.

Tuna becomes dry and tough if overcooked. Cook to medium-rare doneness for best results.

GRILLED CARAMELIZED SALMON AND ASPARAGUS

MAKES 4 SERVINGS

- 1 salmon fillet with skin, 1 inch thick (about 1 pound)
- 2 tablespoons packed brown sugar
- 1 tablespoon grated orange peel
- 1 teaspoon minced garlic
- ½ teaspoon plus ⅛ teaspoon salt, divided
- ⅛ teaspoon ground red pepper
- 16 asparagus spears, trimmed
- 2 teaspoons olive oil
- ¼ teaspoon black pepper
- 1 cup finely chopped fresh pineapple

1. Place salmon, skin side down, in large shallow dish. Combine brown sugar, orange peel, garlic, ½ teaspoon salt and red pepper in small bowl; mix well. Rub mixture over fish. Cover and refrigerate 2 to 8 hours.

2. Prepare grill for direct cooking. Oil grid.

3. Brush asparagus with oil; sprinkle with remaining ⅛ teaspoon salt and black pepper.

4. Grill salmon, skin side down, covered, over medium heat 6 minutes. Place asparagus on grid. Grill, covered, turning asparagus occasionally, 4 minutes or until fish begins to flake when tested with fork and asparagus begins to brown.

5. Cut salmon into four pieces. Top with pineapple; serve with asparagus.

GRILLED HALIBUT WITH CHERRY TOMATO RELISH

MAKES 4 SERVINGS

4 halibut fillets (about 6 ounces each)
2 cloves garlic, minced
3 tablespoons lemon juice, divided
2 teaspoons grated lemon peel, divided
2 teaspoons olive oil, divided
¼ teaspoon salt, divided
¼ teaspoon black pepper, divided
2 cups cherry tomatoes, quartered
2 tablespoons chopped fresh parsley

1. Place halibut in large resealable food storage bag. Combine garlic, 2 tablespoons lemon juice, 1 teaspoon lemon peel, 1 teaspoon oil, ⅛ teaspoon salt and ⅛ teaspoon pepper in small bowl; pour over fish. Seal bag; turn to coat. Marinate in refrigerator 1 hour.

2. Combine tomatoes, parsley, remaining 1 tablespoon lemon juice, 1 teaspoon lemon peel, 1 teaspoon oil, ⅛ teaspoon salt and ⅛ teaspoon pepper in medium bowl; mix well.

3. Prepare grill for direct cooking. Oil grid. Remove fish from marinade; discard marinade.

4. Grill fish 3 to 5 minutes per side or until fish begins to flake when tested with fork. Serve with relish.

MAPLE SALMON AND SWEETS

MAKES 4 SERVINGS

- ½ cup pure maple syrup
- 2 tablespoons butter, melted
- 1½ pounds skin-on salmon fillets
- 2 medium sweet potatoes, peeled and cut crosswise into ¼-inch slices
- 1 teaspoon salt
- ¼ teaspoon black pepper

1. Combine maple syrup and butter in small bowl. Place salmon in large resealable food storage bag. Place sweet potatoes in another large resealable food storage bag. Pour half of syrup mixture into each bag; seal bags and turn to coat. Refrigerate at least 2 hours or overnight, turning bags occasionally.

2. Prepare grill for direct cooking. Oil grid. Drain salmon and sweet potatoes; discard marinade. Season with salt and pepper.

3. Grill fish, skin side down, covered, over medium heat 15 to 20 minutes or until fish begins to flake when tested with fork. (Do not turn.) Grill sweet potatoes, covered, in single layer on grill topper 15 minutes or until tender and slightly browned, turning once.

BLAZING VEGETABLES & SIDES

GRILLED TRI-COLORED PEPPER SALAD

MAKES 4 TO 6 SERVINGS

1   *each* large red, yellow and green bell pepper, cut into halves or quarters

⅓   cup extra virgin olive oil

3   tablespoons balsamic vinegar

2   cloves garlic, minced

¼   teaspoon salt

¼   teaspoon black pepper

⅓   cup crumbled goat cheese

¼   cup thinly sliced fresh basil leaves

1. Prepare grill for direct cooking.

2. Grill bell peppers, skin side down, covered, over high heat 10 to 12 minutes or until skin is blackened. Place peppers in brown paper bag; close bag and let stand 10 to 15 minutes. Remove from bag; peel off charred skin.

3. Place bell peppers in shallow serving dish. Whisk oil, vinegar, garlic, salt and black pepper in small bowl until well blended. Pour over roasted peppers; let stand 30 minutes at room temperature. (Or cover and refrigerate up to 24 hours. Bring to room temperature before serving.) Sprinkle with goat cheese and basil just before serving.

CHILI-RUBBED GRILLED VEGETABLE KABOBS

MAKES 4 SERVINGS

2 ears corn, husked and cut into 1-inch pieces

1 red bell pepper, cut into 12 (1-inch) pieces

1 yellow bell pepper, cut into 12 (1-inch) pieces

1 green bell pepper, cut into 12 (1-inch) pieces

1 medium sweet or red onion, cut into 12 wedges

2 tablespoons olive oil

1 teaspoon seasoned salt

1 teaspoon chili powder

½ teaspoon sugar

1. Alternately thread corn, bell peppers and onion onto 12-inch metal skewers; brush with oil.

2. Combine seasoned salt, chili powder and sugar in small bowl; sprinkle over all sides of vegetables. Wrap skewers in heavy-duty foil; refrigerate up to 8 hours.

3. Prepare grill for direct cooking.

4. Unwrap skewers; grill over medium heat 10 to 12 minutes or until vegetables are tender, turning occasionally.

PORTOBELLO MUSHROOM BURGER WITH MOZZARELLA

MAKES 4 SERVINGS

⅓ cup olive oil, plus more as needed

2 tablespoons chopped fresh parsley

2 teaspoons red wine vinegar

2 cloves garlic, minced

   Salt and black pepper

4 large portobello mushrooms, stems trimmed

4 slices mozzarella cheese

4 thick slices red onion

4 kaiser or rustic rolls, split

2 cups DOLE® Leafy Romaine

4 tablespoons light mayonnaise or other favorite condiment

1. Mix oil, parsley, vinegar and garlic in shallow dish; season with salt and pepper. Add mushrooms and turn to coat thoroughly.

2. Grill mushrooms over medium-high heat, turning often until just cooked through, 7 to 10 minutes; top with mozzarella and cook 2 minutes more. Lightly brush onion slices with olive oil or any remaining marinade and grill, turning once, about 5 minutes. Toast the rolls, cut side down, on grill.

3. Place one mushroom on bottom of each roll. Top each with grilled onion and romaine. Spread mayonnaise on cut side of roll tops and place on burgers. Serve with vegetable chips.

GRILLED VEGGIES AND COUSCOUS

MAKES 4 TO 6 SERVINGS

⅓ cup pine nuts

1½ cups chicken broth or water

2 tablespoons olive oil, divided

½ teaspoon salt

1 cup uncooked couscous

1 medium zucchini, cut lengthwise into ½-inch slices

1 medium red bell pepper, cut in half

½ small red onion, sliced

¼ cup crumbled feta cheese

1 clove garlic, minced

½ teaspoon lemon-pepper seasoning

Salt and black pepper

1. Spread pine nuts in small skillet. Cook and stir over medium heat 4 minutes or until lightly browned.

2. Combine broth, 1 tablespoon oil and ½ teaspoon salt in small saucepan; bring to a boil over medium-high heat. Stir in couscous. Remove from heat; cover and set aside.

3. Prepare grill for direct cooking. Brush vegetables with remaining 1 tablespoon oil.

4. Grill zucchini and onion 3 to 5 minutes or until tender. Grill bell pepper 7 to 10 minutes or until skin is blackened. Place pepper in brown paper bag; close bag and let stand 5 minutes. Remove from bag; peel off charred skin. Chop vegetables.

5. Spoon couscous into serving bowl; fluff with fork. Add vegetables, pine nuts, cheese, garlic and lemon-pepper seasoning. Season with salt and black pepper; toss gently.

GRILLED VEGETABLE PIZZAS

MAKES 4 MAIN-DISH OR 8 APPETIZER SERVINGS

2 tablespoons olive oil

1 clove garlic, minced

1 red bell pepper, cut into quarters

4 slices red onion, cut ¼ inch thick

1 medium zucchini, halved lengthwise

1 medium yellow squash, halved lengthwise

1 cup prepared pizza sauce

¼ teaspoon red pepper flakes

2 (10-inch) prepared pizza crusts

2 cups (8 ounces) shredded fontinella or mozzarella cheese

¼ cup sliced fresh basil leaves

1. Prepare grill for direct cooking.

2. Combine oil and garlic in small bowl; brush over bell pepper, onion, zucchini and yellow squash.

3. Grill vegetables, covered, over medium heat 10 minutes or until crisp-tender, turning halfway through grilling time.

4. Cut bell pepper lengthwise into ¼-inch strips. Cut zucchini and squash crosswise into ¼-inch slices. Separate onion slices into rings.

5. Combine pizza sauce and red pepper flakes in small bowl; spread over crusts. Top with cheese and grilled vegetables.

6. Grill pizzas, covered, over medium-low heat 5 to 6 minutes or until hot. Sprinkle with basil; cut into wedges.

EASY SUMMER VEGETABLE MEDLEY

MAKES 4 TO 6 SERVINGS

2 medium red or green bell peppers, cut into chunks

2 medium zucchini or summer squash, sliced lengthwise in half and then into thick slices

1 (12-ounce) package mushrooms, cleaned and cut into quarters

3 carrots, thinly sliced

1⅓ cups FRENCH'S® French Fried Onions or FRENCH'S® Cheddar French Fried Onions

¼ cup fresh basil, minced

2 tablespoons olive oil

Salt and black pepper to taste

2 ice cubes

1 large foil oven roasting bag

1. Toss all ingredients in large bowl. Open foil bag; spoon mixture into bag in even layer. Seal bag with tight double folds. Place bag on baking sheet.

2. Place bag on grill over medium-high heat. Cover grill and cook 15 minutes until vegetables are tender, turning bag over once.

3. Return bag to baking sheet and carefully cut top of bag open. Sprinkle with additional French Fried Onions, if desired.

PREP TIME: 10 minutes
COOK TIME: 15 minutes

GRILLED SESAME ASPARAGUS

MAKES 4 SERVINGS

1 pound medium asparagus spears (about 20), trimmed

2 teaspoons vegetable oil

1 tablespoon sesame seeds

2 to 3 teaspoons balsamic vinegar

¼ teaspoon salt

¼ teaspoon black pepper

1. Prepare grill for direct cooking. Oil grid.

2. Place asparagus on baking sheet. Drizzle with oil and sprinkle with sesame seeds; roll to coat.

3. Grill asparagus 2 to 3 minutes per side or until beginning to brown. Remove to serving platter.

4. Sprinkle with vinegar, salt and pepper.

JAMAICAN GRILLED SWEET POTATOES

MAKES 6 SERVINGS

- 2 large sweet potatoes (about 1½ pounds)
- 3 tablespoons packed brown sugar
- 3 tablespoons melted butter, divided
- 1 teaspoon ground ginger
- 1 tablespoon chopped fresh cilantro
- 2 teaspoons dark rum

1. Pierce potatoes in several places with fork. Place on paper towel in microwave oven. Microwave on HIGH 5 to 6 minutes or until crisp-tender, rotating one quarter turn halfway through cooking time. Let stand 10 minutes. Cut potatoes diagonally into ¾-inch slices.

2. Combine brown sugar, 1 tablespoon butter and ginger in small bowl; mix well. Stir in cilantro and rum.

3. Prepare grill for direct cooking. Lightly brush one side of each potato slice with half of remaining melted butter.

4. Grill potato slices, butter side down, covered, over medium heat 4 to 6 minutes or until grillmarked. Brush tops with remaining melted butter. Turn and grill 3 to 5 minutes or until grillmarked. Spoon rum mixture over potatoes.

SZECHUAN GRILLED MUSHROOMS

MAKES 4 SERVINGS

1 pound large mushrooms

2 tablespoons soy sauce

2 teaspoons peanut or vegetable oil

1 teaspoon dark sesame oil

1 clove garlic, minced

½ teaspoon crushed Szechuan peppercorns or red pepper flakes

1. Place mushrooms in large resealable food storage bag. Combine soy sauce, peanut oil, sesame oil, garlic and Szechuan peppercorns in small bowl; pour over mushrooms. Seal bag; turn to coat. Marinate at room temperature 15 minutes.

2. Prepare grill for direct cooking. Thread mushrooms onto skewers.

3. Grill mushrooms 10 minutes or until lightly browned, turning once. Serve immediately.

VARIATION: Add 4 green onions, cut into 1½-inch pieces, to marinade. Alternately thread onto skewers with mushrooms. Proceed as directed in Step 2.

SOUTHERN SPICY GRILLED CORN

MAKES 4 SERVINGS

- ½ cup HELLMANN'S® or BEST FOODS® Real Mayonnaise
- 2 tablespoons chopped onion
- 1 tablespoon apple cider vinegar
- ½ tablespoon finely chopped garlic
- ½ teaspoon chipotle powder
- 4 ears corn-on-the-cob, halved

1. In small bowl, combine all ingredients except corn.

2. Grill corn, brushing frequently with mayonnaise mixture, until corn is tender. Garnish, if desired, with chopped fresh cilantro or parsley.

PREP TIME: 8 minutes
COOK TIME: 8 minutes

ACKNOWLEDGMENTS

The publisher would like to thank the companies and organizations listed below for the use of their recipes and photographs in this publication.

Campbell Soup Company

The Coca-Cola Company®

Dole Food Company, Inc.

National Turkey Federation

Ortega®, A Division of B&G Foods North America, Inc.

Reckitt Benckiser LLC.

Recipes courtesy of the Reynolds Kitchens

Unilever

METRIC CONVERSION CHART

VOLUME MEASUREMENTS (dry)

$1/8$ teaspoon = 0.5 mL
$1/4$ teaspoon = 1 mL
$1/2$ teaspoon = 2 mL
$3/4$ teaspoon = 4 mL
1 teaspoon = 5 mL
1 tablespoon = 15 mL
2 tablespoons = 30 mL
$1/4$ cup = 60 mL
$1/3$ cup = 75 mL
$1/2$ cup = 125 mL
$2/3$ cup = 150 mL
$3/4$ cup = 175 mL
1 cup = 250 mL
2 cups = 1 pint = 500 mL
3 cups = 750 mL
4 cups = 1 quart = 1 L

VOLUME MEASUREMENTS (fluid)

1 fluid ounce (2 tablespoons) = 30 mL
4 fluid ounces ($1/2$ cup) = 125 mL
8 fluid ounces (1 cup) = 250 mL
12 fluid ounces ($1 1/2$ cups) = 375 mL
16 fluid ounces (2 cups) = 500 mL

WEIGHTS (mass)

$1/2$ ounce = 15 g
1 ounce = 30 g
3 ounces = 90 g
4 ounces = 120 g
8 ounces = 225 g
10 ounces = 285 g
12 ounces = 360 g
16 ounces = 1 pound = 450 g

DIMENSIONS

$1/16$ inch = 2 mm
$1/8$ inch = 3 mm
$1/4$ inch = 6 mm
$1/2$ inch = 1.5 cm
$3/4$ inch = 2 cm
1 inch = 2.5 cm

OVEN TEMPERATURES

250°F = 120°C
275°F = 140°C
300°F = 150°C
325°F = 160°C
350°F = 180°C
375°F = 190°C
400°F = 200°C
425°F = 220°C
450°F = 230°C

BAKING PAN SIZES

Utensil	Size in Inches/Quarts	Metric Volume	Size in Centimeters
Baking or Cake Pan (square or rectangular)	$8 \times 8 \times 2$	2 L	$20 \times 20 \times 5$
	$9 \times 9 \times 2$	2.5 L	$23 \times 23 \times 5$
	$12 \times 8 \times 2$	3 L	$30 \times 20 \times 5$
	$13 \times 9 \times 2$	3.5 L	$33 \times 23 \times 5$
Loaf Pan	$8 \times 4 \times 3$	1.5 L	$20 \times 10 \times 7$
	$9 \times 5 \times 3$	2 L	$23 \times 13 \times 7$
Round Layer Cake Pan	$8 \times 1 1/2$	1.2 L	20×4
	$9 \times 1 1/2$	1.5 L	23×4
Pie Plate	$8 \times 1 1/4$	750 mL	20×3
	$9 \times 1 1/4$	1 L	23×3
Baking Dish or Casserole	1 quart	1 L	—
	$1 1/2$ quart	1.5 L	—
	2 quart	2 L	—